/22

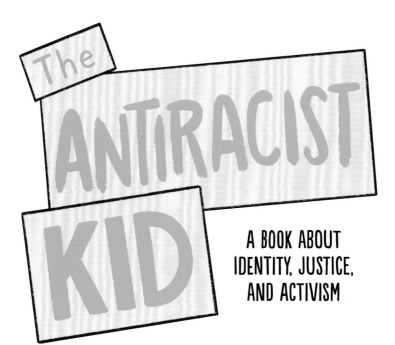

The ANTIRACIST KID

A BOOK ABOUT IDENTITY, JUSTICE, AND ACTIVISM

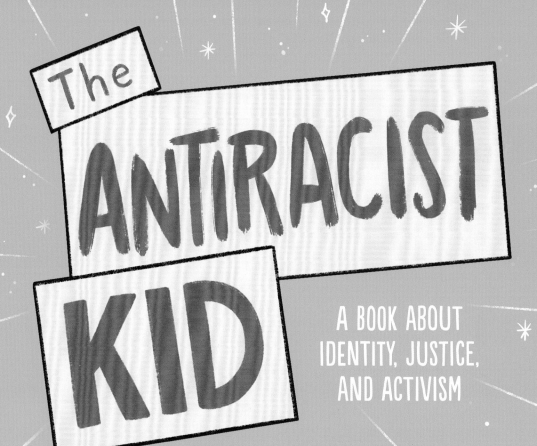

The ANTIRACIST KID

A BOOK ABOUT IDENTITY, JUSTICE, AND ACTIVISM

BY TIFFANY JEWELL

ILLUSTRATED BY NICOLE MILES

▼ VERSIFY

AN IMPRINT OF HARPERCOLLINSPUBLISHERS

Versify® is an imprint of HarperCollins Publishers.

The Antiracist Kid
Text copyright © 2022 by Tiffany Jewell
Illustrations copyright © 2022 by Nicole Miles
All rights reserved. Manufactured in Italy. No part of this book may be used or reproduced in any manner whatsoever
without written permission except in the case of brief quotations embodied in critical articles and reviews. For
information address HarperCollins Children's Books, a division of HarperCollins Publishers, 195 Broadway, New York,
NY 10007.
www.harpercollinschildrens.com

ISBN 978-0-35-862939-9 paper over board
ISBN 978-0-35-862334-2 signed edition

The illustrations in this book were done digitally.
The text was set in Neutraface Text.
Cover design by Samira Iravani
Interior design by Samira Iravani

22 23 24 25 26 RTLO 10 9 8 7 6 5 4 3 2 1

First Edition

For J and S and all the kids (still young and now grown)
who have ever asked big questions

–TJ

For Sage, Chiji, Obi, Ozi, Renzo, Eole, and Amara

–NM

To the ReaDeR

Dear Reader,

Thank you for choosing this book! I wrote this for you. I hope this book helps you to become the antiracist kid you are!

My name is Tiffany. I am a teacher, a mama, and an antiracist adult. I grew up in a city called Syracuse, New York. I lived with my twin sister and my mom. (I really love having a twin sister!) I am a Black, biracial, cisgender woman and a Person of the Global Majority. (We will learn all about what all of these words mean later in this book!)

I have been a teacher for a long time, and I love working with people your age. You are amazing! You are curious. You want to know more about the world around you. You want to know why and how things happen. You are a really good problem solver, and you can help us adults find ways to make the world a much better place to live in for everyone!

When I teach, I hear kids just like you say that they want to take action and make a difference, but sometimes the adults in their lives are not ready for them to do that. I want to tell you that you are never too young to advocate against racism and injustice. Being antiracist is not just work for adults to do. Everyone can be antiracist—especially you and your friends!

In this book, I want to help you understand what antiracism is. I will tell you a little bit about what I have learned about being an antiracist person since I started doing this work. I will also answer questions about things you may want to know more about. This book is full of interesting information. We will look at three different big words and what each one means:

*IDENTITY *JUSTICE *ACTIVISM

You will also meet three people in this book who are kids like you! Their names are Ruby, Shawn, and Dani. When I introduce them in the next few pages, we will learn a little bit about who they are. They will also help me answer your questions about being an antiracist kid!

You do not have to read this book from beginning to end like many other books. You can start reading at the part that looks most interesting to you! Parts of this book may make you feel excited or angry or sad. Parts of this book may make you feel confused. If there is anything in this book that you do not understand, ask the older people who helped you find this book!

The words we use and the way we understand them can grow and change just like people. You will notice that some of the words I use in this book are ones you may already know and use every day. And some of the words may be new to you, ones that you have never heard of or used before. The words we use, the way we say things, and how we communicate (tell and share) with other people have **power**. Words can include or exclude people. They can make us feel happy, like we have power, and they can make us feel sad, like we do not have power. The words we use matter. They are important. The things we say and the thoughts we communicate with our faces and bodies have a big impact on the people around us. In this book, I try to use words that are inclusive because I believe we can all be antiracist together.

I believe that you will help to make this an antiracist world. I am excited to work with you, antiracist kid!

In solidarity,
Tiffany

CONTENTS